SCIENCE ANSWERS

Life Processes

FROM REPRODUCTION TO RESPIRATION

Heinemann Library
Chicago, Illinois

Louise and Richard Spilsbury

Design: Richard Parker and Celia Floyd
Picture Research: Rebecca Sodergren
 and Pete Morris
Originated by Dot Gradations Ltd.
Printed in China by WKT
 Company Limited

08 07 06 05 04
10 9 8 7 6 5 4 3 2 1

Library of Congress Cataloging-in-Publication Data
Spilsbury, Louise.
 Life processes : from reproduction to respiration / Louise Spilsbury and Richard Spilsbury.
      v. cm. -- (Science answers)
 Includes bibliographical references and index.
   Contents: What are life processes? -- What is reproduction? -- How do living things grow? -- How do living things feed? -- What is respiration? -- How do living things get rid of waste? -- Can all living things move? -- What are senses? -- People who found the answers -- Amazing facts.
  ISBN 1-4034-4767-5 (lib. bdg. : hardcover) -- ISBN 1-4034-5513-9 (paperback)
 1. Physiology--Juvenile literature. 2. Reproduction--Juvenile literature. 3. Respiration--Juvenile literature. [1. Physiology. 2. Reproduction. 3. Respiration.] I. Spilsbury, Richard. II. Title. III. Series.
  QP37.S725 2004
  571--dc22

                              2003025664

Acknowledgments
The author and publishers are grateful to the following for permission to reproduce copyright material:

p.4 Corbis; pp.5, 22 Minden Pictures/FLPA; p.6 Science Pictures Limited/Science Picture Library; p.7 Dr. Jeremy Burgess/Science Photo Library; p.8 Martin Harvey/NHPA; p.9 Robert Lifson/Harcourt Education Ltd.; p.10 Gusto/Science Photo Library; p.11 Gregory Ochocki/Science Photo Library; p.12 Stephen Dalton/NHPA; p.13 Terry Andrewartha/FLPA; pp.14, 23, 27 Tudor Photography/Harcourt Education Ltd.; p.15 Wally McNamee/Corbis; p.16 Sunset/FLPA; p.17 Andrew Syred/Science Photo Library; p.18 Peter Chadwick/Science Photo Library; pp.19, 21 Anthony Bannister/NHPA; p.20 Lynwood Chase/Science Photo Library; p.24 Adam Hart-Davis/Science Photo Library; p.25 R. Van Nostrand/FLPA; p.26 John Mitchell/Science Photo Library; p.28 James King-Holmes/Science Photo Library; p.29 Nature Picture Library.

Cover photograph reproduced with permission of Martin Harvey/Corbis.

Every effort has been made to contact copyright holders of any material reproduced in this book. Any omissions will be rectified in subsequent printings if notice is given to the publisher.

Some words are shown in bold, **like this.** You can find out what they mean by looking in the glossary.

Contents

About the demonstrations

This book contains some sections called Science Answers. Each one describes a demonstration that you can try yourself. There are some simple safety rules to follow when doing a demonstration:

- Ask an adult to help with any cutting that uses a sharp knife.
- Wash your hands after handling plants or soil.

Materials you will use

Most of the demonstrations in this book can be done with objects that you can find in your own home. You might also need to buy some supplies at a garden center. You will also need a pencil and paper to record your results.

What Are Life Processes?

Life processes are characteristics that most living things share. They use these processes to live and thrive. Living things on Earth look and behave very differently, but most of them carry out seven basic life processes.

The seven life processes

Below are the seven life processes:

- movement: the ability to move
- **cellular respiration:** the process by which **organisms** release energy from their food
- sensitivity: the process of detecting and responding to changes in the environment
- growth: the process of getting bigger and developing
- **reproduction:** the process of producing offspring
- **excretion:** the process of releasing waste products to keep healthy
- **nutrition:** the process of getting and using food

Living and nonliving

Cars and buses move and excrete waste from their exhaust pipes, but they are not living things. They do not carry out many of the seven life processes.

Not just one

If something carries out one of the life processes, this does not necessarily mean that it is a living thing. For example, sugar crystals can grow in the bottom of a syrup container. However, the crystals do not carry out any of the other life processes. This means that they are not living things.

Cells carry out life processes

All living things are made up of **cells.** Cells are the building blocks of life. Each cell is capable of carrying out life processes such as taking in food, growing, and reproducing. Some organisms such as amoebas are made up of only one cell. Large, more complex organisms such as humans and trees are made up of many cells. Some cells in larger organisms have particular features so that they can perform specific life processes. For example, many animals have muscle cells that help them move.

Dead or alive?

While the corals at the top of a reef may look dead, they are actually alive. However, they are growing on top of dead corals. The corals at the bottom of some coral reefs are more than 3,000 years old.

5

What Is Reproduction?

Every **species** can make new **organisms** similar to themselves. This is called **reproduction.** Without reproduction, all species would die out. Reproduction happens in different ways in different species.

How can a single parent reproduce?

Reproduction involving one parent is called **asexual reproduction.** Part of the parent breaks off, or a bud grows on its surface and then drops off. The new piece, or bud, develops into an identical copy of the parent.

A baby hydra

A hydra is a small animal made up of a few cells. Hydras live in water. In this picture you can see a new hydra budding off from the left side of the larger hydra. This is an example of asexual reproduction.

Asexual reproduction happens in a wide range of simple organisms made up of one or just a few **cells.** For example, single-celled **bacteria** reproduce by splitting in two. Asexual reproduction also happens in more complicated organisms such as plants. For example, strawberry plants produce long shoots with small new plants attached. Once the new plant takes root in the soil, it separates from its parent.

Merging together

Sexual reproduction happens when special cells from a male and a female of the same species join to make a new organism. This new organism is not exactly like either of its parents, but it shows characteristics of both of them. In animals, male **sex cells** are called sperm and female sex cells are called eggs. When a male sex cell and a female sex cell join together in a process called **fertilization,** a new cell is created. The cell then starts to grow into a new individual.

Fertilization happens in flowering plants by **pollination.** This is when male sex cells, called **pollen,** move from the male parts of a flower to the female parts of the same or another flower. The pollen fertilizes an egg that grows into a seed. The seed may eventually grow into a new plant.

Passing pollen

Pollen may be blown by the wind, washed along by water, or carried by insects and birds from flower to flower. Honeybees accidentally pick up pollen on their bodies when they visit flowers to feed on **nectar.**

Fertilization in animals

Male animals **fertilize** eggs either outside or inside the females. Female fish and frogs lay many eggs in water. Males then spray their sperm onto the eggs. Male **mammals,** birds, and insects put their sperm inside the female. This is called mating.

Hatching

Some baby animals such as crocodiles hatch out of eggs that their mothers have laid. Mammals grow safely inside their mothers' bodies. Mammals also make milk and care for their babies after they are born.

Successful reproduction

Reproduction is successful if fertilized eggs grow into new adults capable of reproduction. Living things use different ways of making sure reproduction is successful. For example, flowers look colorful, smell good, and make sweet **nectar** to attract animals that will carry off their **pollen.** Seeds protect the new plant inside from damage and provide a source of food to help it grow. Flowers often make many seeds so that at least a few will succeed.

How Do Living Things Grow and Develop?

Some living things grow by increasing the number of **cells** that they have and by increasing the size of their cells.

More cells

Many **organisms** start growing as soon as they are formed. They get the energy their cells need to divide and grow from food. First, a cell divides in two and each smaller identical cell increases in size. Then the two cells divide into four, four into eight, and so on.

As the number of cells increases, some cells change in order to take on different tasks for the organism. For example, cells of the same type work together in **tissues** such as muscle. Several kinds of tissues make up **organs** such as the heart in some animals or leaves in plants. These body parts help carry out particular life processes.

Getting bigger

All living things grow. As hermit crabs grow, they find bigger shells of dead sea snails to live in. They do not form their own **exoskeletons** like other crabs do.

Genes and growth

Young **organisms** grow to be like their parent or parents because of the **genes** passed on in **reproduction.** Genes are like a **cell's** instruction manual that tells it how it should grow. New individuals produced by **asexual reproduction** have genes that are the same as their their parent's. Young organisms produced by **sexual reproduction** grow from a cell that contains genes from both parents.

Growing and changing

Frogs start life as tadpoles that live in water. As the tadpoles' cells divide and grow, they form different body parts. The tadpoles eventually change into frogs that live on land.

Ways of growing

Organisms grow in different ways. Some animals, such as fox cubs, look like small versions of their parents. Other organisms change in appearance as they grow. For example, the tadpoles that hatch from frogs' eggs look nothing like the adult frogs they will become. Some organisms, such as humans, grow until they are adults and then stop growing. Plants keep growing until they die.

How Do Living Things Feed?

All living things take in food. This process is called **nutrition.** Living things use food to supply the energy that their bodies need to carry out life processes. Plants are called **producers** because they make their own food. Animals are **consumers.** They eat plants or other animals that eat plants.

Plants make food

Plants use **carbon dioxide,** energy from sunlight, and water to make their food. They take in carbon dioxide through holes in their leaves called **stomata.** They take in water through their roots. Plant leaves take in sunlight and use its energy to combine the carbon dioxide and water. The final product is sugar, an energy-rich food. This process is called **photosynthesis.**

Light feeders

Giant kelp is a seaweed that grows in the ocean. Its long, leaflike fronds grow toward the light so that it can carry out photosynthesis. Here, you can see a California sea lion swimming between the enormous fronds.

Energy for animals

Animals cannot make their own food like plants do. They have to eat other things to get the nutrients they need. Herbivores are animals that feed only on plant parts, such as leaves, seeds, berries, and nuts. Carnivores are animals that eat other animals. Some carnivores hunt their prey. For example, many spiders make a sticky web that catches insects for them to eat. Omnivores are animals that eat both plants and animals.

Food chains

The Sun is the source of all energy for living things on Earth. A food chain always begins with green plants because they can trap this energy using **photosynthesis.** The next link in the chain is a herbivore that eats the plants. Then a carnivore eats the herbivore. Sometimes another carnivore eats that carnivore, and so on. Each plant or animal is like a link in the chain. Energy is passed from one link to the next.

How do other organisms feed?

Most **bacteria** use **chemicals** to break down food and then absorb it through their **cell** walls. Some bacteria, called cyanobacteria, make food by photosynthesis like plants do. **Protists,** such as those that form part of the **plankton** in the ocean, make food by photosynthesis, too. Other protists, such as amoebas, surround their **prey** and **digest** it while they have it trapped. **Fungi** such as mushrooms take in **nutrients** from the dead plants and animals they grow on.

Living things need water

The bodies of living things are made up mostly of water. To be healthy and be able to carry out the life processes, most living things need to take in some water every day.

A changing diet

Some animals eat different foods at different stages of life. **Mammals** drink their mothers' milk as babies, but they eat the same food as their parents when they grow older.

DEMONSTRATION: Find out how plants take in water

EQUIPMENT
Celery stalk with the leaves still on, an empty jar, a bottle of food coloring, a knife

STEPS
1. Put an inch of water in the bottom of the jar.
2. Add a few drops of food coloring to the water.
3. Slice a stalk of the celery at the bottom and stand it in the jar of colored water. Leave it in a warm, well lit place for a few days.
4. Check the celery every day and write down what you see.
5. Wash the end of the celery, cut a slice off the bottom of the stem, and look at the slice. Write down what you see.
6. Throw the celery stalk away.

EXPLANATION
All plants need water to make their food. Plants take the water in through their roots and up their stems into their leaves. The colored spots in the cut celery stem are the tubes that the plant uses to carry water up to its leaves. The leaves changed color because the colored water went all the way up the stem.

What Is Cellular Respiration?

Cellular respiration is the process living things use to release the energy from their food. This goes on in every **cell** in an **organism.**

Burning fuel

For a car to work, it has to burn its fuel, gasoline, with **oxygen.** Most living things release energy from their fuel, food, by using oxygen, too. In cellular respiration, sugars from food are combined with oxygen inside the organism's cells. This releases energy that the cells can use to divide and grow, repair themselves, and carry out all the other life processes.

Some organisms, including some **bacteria,** are able to release all of the energy from their food without oxygen.

Releasing energy

When runners race down a track, their muscle cells are using energy released from food by cellular respiration.

15

Breathing

Living things need to take in a constant supply of **oxygen** for **cellular respiration.** Many animals get oxygen by breathing it in. They breathe out to release **carbon dioxide** from their bodies. Carbon dioxide is a waste gas produced by plants and animals in the process of cellular respiration.

Lungs and gills

Living things have different **organs** for obtaining oxygen. Many animals, including humans, have lungs. When humans breathe, muscles in the body force air into the lungs. The lungs take oxygen from the air and the blood carries it to the body's **cells.** Fish have gills with thin **blood vessels** that take in oxygen from the water and push out carbon dioxide.

Blowhole breathing

Killer whales have blowholes on the tops of their heads. They use the blowholes to breathe when they come to the surface of the water.

How do plants get oxygen?

Plants produce some of the oxygen they need for cellular respiration during the process of **photosynthesis.** They also take oxygen in through their **stomata.** This magnified picture shows the stomata on a leaf.

Plants can open and close their stomata using the two cells on either side of the opening. Oxygen for cellular respiration passes into the leaf through the stomata.

Plants also get some of their oxygen from the water that they take in through their roots.

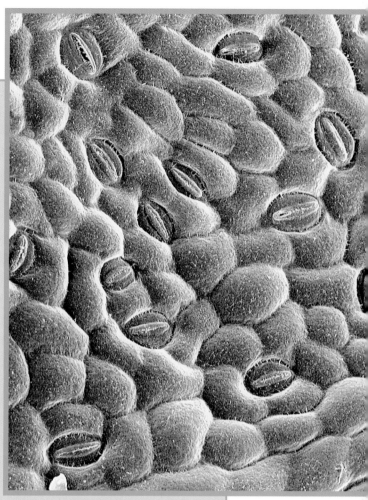

Saving up energy

Plants store some of the food they make in underground plant parts such as roots or underground stems. Potatoes and carrots are plant food stores. When the plant needs energy to grow again in the spring, it uses cellular respiration to release energy from the stored food.

How Do Living Things Get Rid of Waste?

All living things produce waste when they carry out life processes in their **cells.** Some of the waste can be harmful or even poisonous if it builds up. **Excretion,** the way a living thing gets rid of waste, is an important life process.

Getting rid of liquid waste

Living things need different **nutrients** such as fats, water, and **proteins.** For example, cells need protein to grow and repair themselves. When cells use protein, they use some parts of it but not others, leaving some waste. Urea is a waste protein. In animals such as fish and **mammals,** urea is excreted mostly by the kidneys. The kidneys are **organs** that take waste and unwanted water out of the blood. Urine is the mixture of water and urea that mammals release.

Plants also produce waste from **nutrition.** Many trees move this waste into the cells of old leaves. The waste is disposed of when the leaves drop off.

Animal waste

This kelp gull in South Africa is standing on a rock stained by guano. Guano is the waste produced by seabirds. It is a thick paste that contains uric acid.

Solid waste

Animals such as mammals also produce solid waste called feces. Feces contain the parts of an **organism's** food such as fiber that cannot be **digested.**

Waste gases

The **carbon dioxide** released during the process of **cellular respiration** could poison living things if it remained in their bodies. Insects excrete carbon dioxide through holes on the sides of their bodies called spiracles. Many animals use gills or lungs. When these animals breathe out, they get rid of the carbon dioxide.

Recycling waste

Waste from one organism is often used by other organisms. For example, when green plants make sugars during **photosynthesis,** they also excrete **oxygen.** Most living things use this oxygen to release energy from their food.

Dung beetles roll feces, or dung, underground to lay their eggs on. The young dung beetles that hatch eat some of the dung. Most of the dung rots, releasing nutrients into the soil that other organisms can use.

Can All Living Things Move?

Most living things have the ability to move. It may be difficult to see **organisms** such as plants moving, but it does happen.

How do plants move?

Plants mainly move as they grow. Plant parts such as branches, roots, and flowers move as they grow. Petals on some flowers close up at night. This protects the delicate parts inside the flower that are used for **reproduction. Pollen** from plants is blown by the wind or carried on the backs of insects such as bees. Most seeds have some way of moving away from their parent plant so that they can find space to grow. Some seeds grow in fruits that are eaten and carried away by animals.

Parachuting seeds

Dandelion seeds have tops that act like tiny parachutes. They carry the seeds through the air even in a very weak breeze.

A plant that moves fast

Most plant movement is so slow and gradual that we cannot see it happening. However, the Venus's flytrap is an unusual plant that can move quite quickly. When an insect lands on its leaves, they shut, trapping the **prey** inside the plant. The Venus's flytrap then **digests** the fly so that it can absorb **nutrients.** The Venus's flytrap cannot usually get these nutrients from the soils in which it grows.

Why do animals move?

Animals move mainly to carry out the other life processes. For example, most have to move to find or catch their food. They move in order to find a partner for reproduction or to get food for their young. Animals also move to escape danger. For example, rabbits run to escape being caught by foxes. Some animals move in special ways that are suited to where they live. The Peringuey's adder, a kind of snake pictured here, travels quickly across the desert using a special S-shaped movement. This keeps most of its body off the burning sand.

How do animals move?

Animals move in many different ways. Humans and many other animals have muscles that pull on the bones in their skeletons to make their bodies move. Animals without bones move in different ways. An earthworm's muscles lengthen and shorten its body to make it move, while hairs on its body grip the soil. Muscles in a jellyfish open and close its body, taking in water and then pushing it out again to propel the jellyfish forward.

How do other organisms move?

Protists such as amoebas move by stretching their bodies across a surface. Other protists have one thin, long hair or many hairs that they move back and forth to swim. Parts of **fungi** move as they grow. For example, a toadstool has a mass of threads that grows out of its base into dead wood and leaves.

How do birds fly?

Birds such as these flamingos have muscles in their bodies that pull on their wing bones to help them fly.

DEMONSTRATION: See how plant parts move

EQUIPMENT
A glass jar, a paper towel, a bean seed (such as a lima bean) that has been soaked in water for a day

STEPS
1. Wet the paper towel with water. Fold it and wrap it around the inside of the jar.
2. Slide the bean down between the inside of the jar and the paper towel so you can see it from the outside of the glass jar.
3. Stand the jar on a windowsill and leave it for a week or two. Keep the paper damp by adding a few drops of water every day if necessary.
4. Write down what you see.

EXPLANATION
When the bean seed starts to grow, its root grows from one end and a shoot grows from the other end. The bean may stay still, but the root moves down the inside of the jar and the shoot moves up the jar as it grows. This proves that plant parts can move.

23

What Are Senses?

Sensitivity is a living thing's ability to detect and respond to things in the world around it. Humans have five senses—sight, hearing, smell, taste, and touch—that help them respond to the world.

Plant sensitivity

Plants react to fewer **stimuli** than humans and other animals, but they clearly do respond to their surroundings. When a seed starts to grow, it does not matter which way up it landed in the soil. Its roots always grow down, and its shoot always grows up. Plants respond to gravity. Plant roots grow down into the soil where they will be able to get the water the plant needs. Meanwhile, plant stems grow up out of the soil where they will be able to hold their leaves up to the Sun for **photosynthesis.**

Reaching for the light

These young tomato plants are leaning over to one side because they are growing toward the light.

Do plants have a sense of touch?

Some climbing plants have a sense of touch. If their stem touches another plant or other possible support, they wrap around it. This allows the climbing plant to grow up toward the light without growing strong stems for support.

Animal senses

The **organs** responsible for the five human senses are the eyes, ears, nose, taste buds, and skin. Most animals have some or all of these sense organs. Most sense organs are on the head. They are close to the brain, which interprets the information collected by the senses. For example, your eyes see a car coming and pass the information to your brain. Your brain tells you it is not safe to cross the road. Messages from sense organs travel to the brain through **nerves.**

Night vision

Animals that are active at night, such as this slender loris, have large eyes to help them see.

Using animal senses

Animals use their senses to do many things such as finding food or escaping danger. Different animals rely on different senses as their main source of information.

Bats find food in the dark by **echolocation.** They make high squeaks that humans cannot hear and listen to the echoes to figure out where an insect is. Some rattlesnakes have heat-sensing **cells** on their heads that help them find warm-bodied **prey,** such as mice, in the dark. Fish and tadpoles have a line of cells along their sides that sense movements in the water. It tells them if food or danger is nearby. Cats' whiskers help them feel their way around in the dark.

What are antennae?

Insect antennae are **organs** that touch, smell, and taste. Male luna moths like this one have very large antennae. The antennae pick up a smell that females give off.

DEMONSTRATION: Show that plants sense and respond to light

EQUIPMENT
Cardboard box, stiff cardboard, tape, scissors, a young lima bean plant with two leaves that is growing in a small pot, pencil, paper

STEPS
1. Tape pieces of cardboard inside the box to create a maze like the one in the picture.
2. Stand the box up, put the plant at the bottom, make a hole in the top, and put the lid on tight.
3. Stand the box in a sunny place. Take the lid off once a day for three weeks to check the plant. Water the plant if necessary. Write down what you see.

EXPLANATION
After one to three weeks, the lima bean grows around the obstacles and out of the hole at the top of the box. Plant stems sense and then grow toward sunlight. Their leaves need sunlight to be able to make food.

Gregor Mendel (1822–1884)

Mendel (shown here) was an Austrian **monk** who noticed that sweet pea seeds grew into plants that looked partly like each parent plant. By **pollinating** many sweet pea flowers with each other, he figured out the way in which characteristics of parents are passed on to their young. Many years after his death, Mendel's writings about his experiments were used by other scientists to study the way that **genes** work.

Anton van Leeuwenhoek (1632–1723)

Leeuwenhoek was born in the Netherlands. He owned a cloth shop, but his hobby was making microscopes. At first he used these homemade microscopes to examine cloth fibers, but he later moved on to leaves, bees, and other living things. He discovered what **cells** in blood, hair, and skin look like close up. Although microscopes had been invented before van Leeuwenhoek, he was the first person to use them for careful scientific study.

Amazing Facts

- The biggest trees in the world are giant sequoias, which can weigh up to 2,500 tons.

- The blue whale (shown here) is the largest animal in the world, weighing as much as 130 tons.

- Some kinds of bamboo can grow nearly 35 inches (90 centimeters) in a single day.

- The oldest living thing in the world is a tree that is almost 4,800 years old!

- Queen army ants may produce three million eggs each month.

- Some aphids (a type of insect that eats plants) take only four days after hatching from eggs to become adults.

- Giant squids have eyes up to 14 inches (35 centimeters) across.

- To keep skin sensitive to touch, human skin cells constantly die, fall off, and are replaced by new ones. Some scientists say humans lose as many as 40,000 dead skin cells every minute!

▷◦ Glossary

asexual reproduction   organism reproduces by creating another living thing from a part of itself

bacterium (more than one are bacteria)   common single-celled organism with no nucleus

blood vessel   tube that carries blood

carbon dioxide   gas found in small amounts in air. Plants use it for photosynthesis and animals breathe it out.

cell   building block of living things that can only be seen with a microscope. Most plants and animals are made up of millions of cells.

cellular respiration   process by which living things release energy from their food

chemical   basic substance that things are made of

consumer   living thing that eats other living things

digest   break down food into nutrients that an organism can use

echolocation   process of finding an object using reflected sound. Bats and dolphins use echolocation to find prey.

excrete   get rid of waste

exoskeleton   hard covering on the outside of an arthropod's body

fertilize   male sex cell joins with a female sex cell

fungus (more than one are fungi)   type of living thing that is not an animal or a plant. Fungi include mushrooms, molds, yeasts, and toadstools.

gene   code carried in a cell that determines how it grows

mammal   kind of animal that feeds its babies milk from its own body and has some hair

monk   person who dedicates his or her life to a religion

nectar   sugary liquid that plants make in their flowers to attract insects and birds

nerve   thin thread that sends messages between the brain and other parts of the body

nutrient   chemical that plants and animals need in order to live

nutrition   process of getting and using food

organ   part of the body that has a particular function

organism   living thing

oxygen   gas in the air which many living things need in order to survive

photosynthesis   process by which plants make their own food using water, carbon dioxide, and energy from sunlight

plankton   group of microscopic organisms that live in the surface waters of the oceans

pollen   small, dustlike particle that contains male sex cells

pollinate   place pollen on the female part of a flower

prey   animal that is caught and eaten by another animal

producer   living thing that makes its own food

protein   chemical that living things need for growth and repair

protist   microscopic organism with a nucleus

reproduction   when a living thing produces young like itself

sex cell   male or female cell that combines to make a young organism

sexual reproduction   organism reproduces by joining a male and a female sex cell

species   group of organisms that have similar characteristics

stimulus (more than one are stimuli)   something that causes a reaction or response

stoma (more than one are stomata)   small opening on a leaf that takes in carbon dioxide and gets rid of oxygen

tissue   group of cells connected together

More Books to Read

DuPrau, Jeanne. *Cells*. Farmington Hills, Mich.: Gale Group, 2001.

Nadeau, Isaac. *Water in Plants and Animals*. New York: Rosen Publishing, 2003.

Riley, Peter. *Senses*. Milwaukee: Gareth Stevens, 2003.

Index